BLACK GIRL EVOLVING II

Journey to Softness

Diana Townsend

Dedication:

I dedicate this book to Black women who have been silenced by society… who have been mistreated and abused, who have been ignored in doctor's offices, who have been told they can handle more pain than others, who have been neglected, who have been ignored, who have been mimicked, and for those who have died without ever truly experiencing a life where their needs came first…

This is for you.

This is for us.

INTRODUCTION

When I was pregnant with my daughter, I would complain about various aches and pains... everyone around me told me I was being dramatic. I remember telling my doctor and nurses that I was leaking fluid... and they told me I was overexaggerating. Then, when they went to break my water, the sac was almost dry. The room went silent, but there was no apology.

I remember every time I tried to advocate for myself, only to be dismissed, invalidated, and unheard. I can think of moments when I calmly stated my claims and was accused of being angry, agitated, and scary. I have self-regulated myself to make others comfortable more times than I can count.

These experiences are not unique or only my own. The more Black women I speak to, the more universal it seems. The soft-life era we have entered is a nice start to changing the structures in place that try to paint us as super-beings who never tire, hurt, or cry... but it's not enough.

Writing books for Black women is part of my therapy. No one can silence my writing or quiet my voice once I put these words on the page. No one can invalidate my feelings or try to gaslight me or women like me who can relate to these experiences. Writing this book and Black Girl Evolving has been freeing for me... and offers me a safe space to say everything I have been holding inside to make others feel comfortable. It ends here... and I rejoice inside every time a Black woman reaches out to me and says,

"Sis... I needed this." So did I, sis. *So did I.*

CONTENTS

CONTENT WARNING

This book contains poems that have triggering themes such as:

- eating disorders or disordered eating
- suicidal thoughts and/or actions
- mental, emotional, sexual, and physical abuse
- trauma
- depression and anxiety

Please prioritize your mental health and read this with the understanding that some of the poems could possibly be triggering for you. Please read with care and caution. Thank you.

CHILDHOOD:
TRAUMA PRINCESS

Little Black girl
didn't you know
good girls don't walk with a sway in their hips
guiding grown men's eyes to your bottom
unknowingly attracting attention from
strangers, uncles, cousins, and neighbors...

Secret pedophiles protected by
good Christian Black women
who would rather shame a child
for a shape she cannot control
that confront the familiar trauma
that has plagued the family
for generations.

Good girls don't tell.
They cry silent tears that fade
like the photographs of their youth...
the good old days
were only good
from certain perspectives.

Summertime
sun on my thighs
feeling free like no one can touch me
I am invincible, young, and Black
as I swing from the roped tire hanging from the low branch
gliding through the air
screaming with abandon
our dog barks in anticipation
my sisters listening out for the ice cream truck
my parents, inside, avoiding each other
but not arguing,
at least not today, not at this moment...

I allow myself to breathe easily
and feel like a child
for a minute or two.

Girl, close that damn door,
don't let out all my good air
and don't touch my thermostat
cause you don't pay no bills
up in here…

She told me,
if you're really hungry
you'll eat what's on the table
cause you don't have
McDonald's money…

She whispered,
that all men were dogs
and to always have my own
bank account with money stashed away
because a man was the worst thing
to depend on…

I listened, mama.
I listened.

And you were right.

Swinging, swinging
feet back and forth
sun on my brown face
pigtails with pink and purple barrettes on the ends...
I remember the call that the birds would sing
to one another
while the world slowly began to awaken
and our gated swing set
was a safe haven
a fortress
my gateway to the clouds...
The one place where I could be
a child
free from the worries
of the world
for a little while.

I took the rides
and went to the car windows
my little self
admitting my age and seeing the nonchalance
it felt so cool, back then, to be wanted
and it doesn't haunt me until
I shower and feel the hands
of grown men
stroking me
and I scrub and scrub and scrub
until my flesh is raw and pained...

I took the rides
and went to the car windows...
my little self.

Reading class was my home
my safe space
the only castle befitting a queen
of my stature
for words were the fluid
that ignited my veins
until my 12th-grade English teacher
gave me zeros in her green binder
where she kept her obsolete grades
because I refused to recite a poem
she had chosen for me...
I kept the pain close to my heart
as she wrote the zeros in the book
and the students laughed as she sang,
"Zero city... she's going to zero city!"
and I bit my tongue until it bled
because teachers like her
could make or break
students like me.

I was, what they call,
an emotional child
immature and whiny
dramatic and silly...
I would commiserate in my dark room,
and confide in my teddy bears
that one day,
I would be a big star
and I would never let people forget
how they treated me.

The snide remarks
the whispered jokes
the pinches of my flesh between fingers...

No one knew that I stuffed my tummy
late at night
with lukewarm soup and stale crackers
with sandwiches and cheese toast
with cookies and candy...
stuffed to the edge of pain
eating to fill a void,
to put me to sleep,
to make me forget.

It's hard to explain
being the oddball,
the weirdo,
the continuous fuck-up,
the sad black sheep…
in a family of beautiful curly-haired girls
and then me…
with my coarse thick hair,
my shapely big body,
my wide nose,
my regular features…
all the wrong people saw my beauty
and I devoured that unfulfilling fruit
but always felt like I was starving
for more.

Popcorn,
arguing over who gets the remote,
running to the bathroom during commercial breaks,
Channel 33 on lock,
the line-up was immaculate,
hushed tones,
lights off,
high-pitched squeals of laughter
and then scared delight...
four girls, safe in their heads
safe in their beds,
for the night.

The first time a man entered me
my vision of childhood slipped away
and I felt like a woman
trapped in a child's body
for being 12 felt too young
to do what I was doing
but he said I was mature,
different from other girls my age...
he said no one would understand if they knew
he *said* that secrets would make us closer
he said *he* loved me...
and I melted into his sheets
hurting but thinking
finally, someone loves me...
right?

He stopped answering my calls
the very next day.

I couldn't see past my own insecurities
the future was blurry
and a lot of my stumbles were
self-inflicted
as I sought out love and acceptance
from men who were old and rotten
who fed me lies wrapped in pretty packages
and I never truly had the chance to learn
who I was and who I could be...
My god, I wish I could've seen it.

One single bottle of pills
that ought to do it
my heart was racing
but at least the bullying and the taunting
would stop...

When I woke up
disoriented and disappointed
I thought, wow... I'm still here
and it was both terrifying and exhilarating
all at the same
time.

Some of us hated high school
for what is there to love
when no one is protecting your
innocence or your education...
I've had teachers bully me
more than any of the students
and I've had peers who
convinced me that I was worthless
because I "thought I was cute"
when I really never thought that
at all.

I just wanted to read my books
and be left alone.

Memories can be the jail
we choose to rot in
and they tell us forgiveness is the key
but I have found that it is more of the blade
in which I would love to use
to slice the throats of my enemies.
That would unlock a sense of peace
for me,
and maybe they would forgive me...
maybe not.

DIANA TOWNSEND

I was the gifted child
who could read well beyond her years
and I consumed books with greediness
for those words allowed me to travel
away from home,
away from my abusers,
away from my family,
away from school,
away from men,
and into worlds of fairies and witches
families with moms and dads who didn't yell and fight
sisters who adored each other
and little girls who were safe and protected
within those hardbound covers.

Teenage dreams
of love and marriage
my heart was convinced that I
would be able to do it differently
and better than everyone around me...
What a young fool I was.

I never had real best friends
and the girls I trusted
should not have been trusted at all...
I have gotten better at observing
before declaring that someone is a friend
and while my phone is dry
and there are no girl trips in my future
that chance of betrayal is much lower
then it was when I was a naïve teen.

Football games...
crisp chilly air
concession stand with lines of cute guys
and flirty girls
chili cheese nachos with strawberry soda
jackets with letters
that one group of boys who never missed a game
but you never saw in class...
sitting with your girls
hair in a cornrow, freeze, or a tree ponytail
fly girls in our own right
nerds in the real world
but the night was young
and so were we.

Bullying is…
the constant threats after school
mean girls spreading rumors and lies
boys grabbing your butt because everyone thinks
you're easy and you like it.

Bullying is…
the red and white bottle of pills I took
in hopes that I would wake up and see Jesus
but instead, I woke up in my pale pink room
disappointed, heart racing, and then
with a shock of relief, understanding
that I'm still here.

I'm still here.

Watermelon mist
pink bubble gum
candy canes in pickles
caramel apple lollipops
the candy lady complaining about Arth'r acting up
and me, eating a fifty cent pack of peanut butter cups
on the way to school
feeling invincible and invisible
all at the same time.

Memories and regret
are like a prison
they will feed you and nourish you
just enough to keep you alive
and going...
the loop is torture
as you watch and watch and watch
wishing you could change one small thing
wishing you could stop one event
wishing you could go back in time
knowing it's time to let it all go...

knowing it's time
to let it all
go.

Eighteen-year-old me would be
severely disappointed
in what I've allowed us to become.
She was, in every way,
full of life and love
beaten but not worn,
and excited about life's possibilities...
despite her trauma.

I failed her, time and time again,
trusting my heart and not my brain,
going against everything I knew to be true,
and some days I can't bear the weight
of her judgment and despair
over what could have been.

DIANA TOWNSEND

Cocoa butter dreams
soft linen sheets
hair in a bonnet
curled in gentle pink rollers while she sleeps...

dream little black girl, dream away
this world has nothing that you need
you are made of the remnants of queens
the minerals from fallen stars
and you are the fiber that holds this place
together.

Dream little black girl,
dream away.

Cheese toast and sweet tea
fuzzy socks with an itchy nightgown
coarse black hair sectioned into five parts
face slick with Vaseline...

I snuggle into my favorite chair
with books stacked high
for this is my safe place
and no one can find me once I get started
for my imagination was stronger than their distractions...

thank God.

Childhood stress leads to traumatized teens
what child should have to worry about having enough
food, love, compassion, or comfort
and yet this is the reality for some...
when your household consists of a single mother
who is not bitter but just exhausted
and trying to survive
her cup is too empty to pour into her children
and there is no village
the foundation is rocky and weak
and all of the lost boys and girls
gather in the streets
engaged in the type of foolishness
that entertains idle minds.

I was a nonchalant child
nothing truly moved me or convinced me
that life was anything special.

This sort of detachment is common
with unmotivated and unchallenged gifted children.

I remember walking to the public library
because no one felt like driving me
and I would spend the thirty minutes there
smile on my face,
the neighborhood boys would trail me on their bikes
until I went too far,
and then I was on my own.

I would get inside and breathe in the cool air
mind you, it was always empty,
and I would take my time and visit every aisle
tracing the covers with my fingertips
reading a little of everything
haunting myself with stories that left a mark
but age has caused me to lose the title.

I would lug my books home
arms heavy but determined not to let them fall
and it never failed that the walk home felt
longer and more exhausting
grown men would hoot and holler from their cars
begging me to let them give me a ride home
and I would shout, "I'm only twelve," with a shy grin
but they did not care…
if anything, it made them beg more.

That part, I cannot forget.

Short skirts
red lipstick
straightened hair
shoes with heels or wedges
painted toes
sweet perfume

a few of my favorite things...

but also, dangerous things
for these were an instant signal that I was grown
or fast for my age
and gave grown men and women the green light
to judge me
to persecute me
to make passes at me
and to harass me.

It was exhausting.

YOUNG ADULTHOOD: LOST AND FOUND

Freshman year was...
curious eyes and lost identity
open legs to frat boys
hard heads and soft behinds
failing classes and missed alarms
scholarships granted and then lost
the harsh reality that no matter the campus
or the distance
one cannot escape the trauma
they choose to avoid.

Moving back home
a failure disguised as a nonchalant rebel
the whispers of disappointment
the realization that
you no longer have a space here
you were never meant to return here
a discarded package with no home address
longing for the answers
or just another chance
to make it right.

Painful cycles
baby lumps
the first fibroid started growing
without me ever knowing
and ignorance was bliss
for a little while...
only for a little while.

I met a man with a boyish charm
when I was twenty years old
and I saw the stars in his eyes
his smile melted my heart
and I abused him in the way
that girls who have only seen toxic love
will do.

I cooked for him
gave him sweet kisses and small smiles
but I kept fighting with him
to keep the sparks alive
because drama fuels true love,
doesn't it?

In a lot of ways,
I was gifted and charming
but also foolish and nonchalant
for I forgot that books were more loyal than men
and I could not outplay them, in their own game
no matter how I tried.

I was not the fly girl I had imagined or read about,
and my ears were still wet and my behind was still soft
and those lessons came hard and fast…

too bad, so sad.

DIANA TOWNSEND

We took trips to the store
picking out things for our imaginary apartment
me and my black sheep boy
he was his family's fuck-up
and so was I...
and we bonded in our eagerness
to prove them all wrong
or to prove ourselves wrong
since we were our own worst critics...
there was no one to blame
for our bad choices
we thirsted for instant gratification
and cried when the consequences came.
It was the most beautiful time of my life
loving this man while he was still innocent and sweet
for I never saw him like that
ever again.

I stopped eating
spontaneously and randomly
one day
I saw myself and knew if I could just be slimmer
my life would change
so I went from three meals and snacks
to two meals and one snack
to one meal and no snacks
to full meals and then a favorite stall
to empty myself for the day
this white girl's disease had found me
and yet life wasn't better...
life wasn't better at all.

Playing with fire is fun
until you get burned
and the ashes reveal every lie
buried beneath good intentions.

One lie I told myself was that this new man
loved me
and the other lie, the more dangerous lie
was that he would be a good father
to our child.

The delusion burned but the truth
it cleared out my soul
and ruined the last of my innocence
for good.

My baby daddy was adorable
the cutest liar you've ever seen
a true narcissist before it became hip
a devil who hid behind roses and gifts
a cheater who would beg for more lunch
he would hug me from behind
caress my pregnant belly
and beg me to make two sandwiches
two drinks and two snacks
only for me to find out he was sharing it
with the woman, he would leave me for...

It's funny now
when I think back on it
how badly I wanted to believe in him
as a man and as a father
but I didn't know that fatherless men
who have not dealt with the trauma of their childhood
will continue to spread the neglect they experienced
and relish in the destruction
of their seed.

Pregnancy was nothing that I thought it would be
and everything that I feared
I learned how to be anxious
the day those tests turned pink
two lines drawing me in
reminding me of how unprotected I was as a child
and forcing me to confront demons
that I long since
tucked away.

Pregnancy while Black can be:
doctors ignoring your aches and pains
people downplaying your emotions
no one coming to your baby shower
wondering what life will be like as a family
crying when he leaves for someone else
going to the WIC office alone
being shamed for using food stamps
questioning what last name to put on the birth certificate
quiet sobs in the middle of the night when the truth comes
to light.

Pregnancy while Black can also be:
luxurious push gifts to celebrate the miracle of life inside of
you
doctors who pay attention to your concerns and birth plans
partners who believe in family and stay by your side
not worrying about finances because you saved and
planned
foot rubs and pregnancy cravings that are met with smiles
private maternity suites with soothing music and views
family photos with matching pajamas
snuggles and kisses while planning for your future family

The choice of partner dictates
which experience
you will have...

Choose wisely.

DIANA TOWNSEND

Discovery of self
is an isolating experience
and we fear a dry phone
more than we fear the beauty
of enjoying our own company.

I often advise young women
to spend their twenties
free from long-term commitments
and babies…

Use that time to explore
the world
yourself
the country
the state
your religion
your spirituality
your sexual desires
and your healing journey.

They usually don't listen
and that's okay
because neither did I.

Neither did I.

Dating was... nonexistent in my mind
because if you called me and we hit it off
then we went together, real bad
and I was all in
while red flags decorated the imaginary home
I made for us with boys at the head of my table...

Careless and rash,
legs opened too quickly
in the name of sexual freedom
giving away a small piece of me
ignorant of the return policy.

Appointments come up
running late, disrespectful of everyone's time
mindlessness leading to distractions
fumbling keys and lost trinkets
stumbling in drunk
2am texts to my least favorite ex…

It feels like rock bottom
but we haven't gotten there,
yet.

The beauty of youth
dwells in the belief
that there are brighter days
ahead...

You have a fire inside of you
a resilience
an unmatched strength that surpasses
years of generational trauma
and drowns the voice of doubt
that whispers in your ear
and tickles your soul
every so often.

Beale Street blues wrapped in the silky film
of gunpowder and sweat
drinking and smoking
not a care in the damn world
just vibes…

We owned the city in those restless summer nights
oblivious to the dangers that lurked in dark alleys
flickin' our cars, four-wheel drive, full speed ahead
demons in our own right
but still up for church service
every Sunday morning…

Southern sluts turned into delicate ladies
dressed in pearls, bibles thumping
hooping and hollerin'
louder than the bass at the club
that we just left.

Young mothers catch so much grief
from their supposed village
and outsiders
who will provide commentary
but not support.

Natural hair shawty
afro as full as the moon
heavy with coconut oil and stardust
silver hoop earrings that graze the shoulder
thick like southern sweet tea
with extra honey
smooth like shea butter
and fresh black soap
plantains and mangoes
this girl…

she was the sample of a hot track
sixteen bars of raw truth
but they were too hard of hearing
to notice.

Back in school, determined to break the chains
single motherhood would not be
the end of my story
and I refused to wear the title
as a badge of shame.

Peace of mind is a luxury
that many of us cannot afford
as we stumble around
unmedicated and refusing therapy
because strong girls don't need help
and our mothers, their mothers, and their mothers,
did it alone,
so why can't we?

The real question is... why should we?

God didn't make anything in this world
that did not require
a little nurturing
to grow.

Success eluded me
mainly because I wouldn't get out
of my own path
blocking my blessings
ignoring the Universe and its signals
I couldn't see greatness in someone
like me
who consistently made bad decisions
and never learned from her mistakes.

It took me too long to see
that redemption isn't given
but it can be earned.

Grace is...
a gorgeous word for mercy
forgiveness in plain clothes
we ask for a measure of grace
with nervous shame
for what person
walking this planet
can assume such power
without hiding their own sins
behind their back?

Money slips and slides through my sticky fingers
spending to fill a void
to ease my incessant search for a sense of stability
and security
worried about running out of food
hoarding to feel safe
spending my time and energy
on everything but
saving for the future.

This is the rat race
of poverty.

One regret that nibbles at my soul
in the darkest hours of the night
is that I never created a home for myself
and experienced the freedom of living alone.

I went from my mother's nest to my marital bed
with very few stops in between
what a luxurious freedom to dwell in
decorating as you please
answering to no one
sitting in peace
watching the shows you enjoy
no children, no partner...
just a sense of seclusion
and independence.

It sounds divine.

My health faded during this time
negligence and fear
avoiding the dentist
but making sure I took my toddler
avoiding the gynecologist
but going to every pediatrician check-up
pouring from an empty mug
a candle lit at both ends
depression filling me with dread
anxiety convincing me that I won't live
to see my daughter turn 18…

Crippled by fear
and doing the absolute best
that I could.

Stumbled into a career
and found my niche
hyper-focused on success
never taking PTO
perfect attendance with imperfect mental health
working towards the perfect image
super mom, super wife, super tired...

I ran myself into the ground
and hit rock bottom
at full speed.

It was an ugly sight
but my social media was perfect
and that's all that mattered
back then.

DIANA TOWNSEND

Mothering did not come natural for me
for I was more of a protector
than a nurturer
and my daughter was protected
but not loved
adequately.

I had four years of enjoying in my twenties
before I became a mother
and one year I was celibate and focused on my future
a different year was spent crying over a boy
the other two are a blur of alcohol and depression…

but I always remember the one where I flourished
watered with self-love and independence
no relationship, no toxic friendships…

I was on my way to somewhere special
until I tripped up and fell in love
with the narcissist that ruined my life
and well…

Excuses play like a scratched record
and skip accountability
regret hangs around my neck like an anchor
and while I know I have to move on …

I just can't.

Warning:

If you stop binging on food
you might replace that addiction
with another addiction
because the food was never truly the problem,
was it?

My hard head often made for a soft behind
many lessons I learned could've been avoided
but my head was full of grand ideas that I was invincible
that I was somehow different and special and immune
to the effects of trauma and abuse.

By the time I realized that I was susceptible to pain
it was too late
and all bets
were off.

WOMANHOOD: FINDING MY WAY HOME

The week of Thanksgiving
I sunk to my lowest low
and I stayed there... for a while.

I pondered life and the meaning behind it
stewed over my past mistakes and sacrifices
forced myself to see how I had become a doormat
in my own life...

Somehow, I picked myself up from the rubble
dusted myself off and picked out the shards of glass
and I learned how to reimagine my life
how to manifest greatness
how to find my voice again
and I taught everyone in my life
how to treat me and how to love me.

For I had learned how to do both,
how to love myself and how to treat myself,
finally.

Friendships ended but I didn't mourn
my marriage took a hit or two but we kept going
and I found my identity outside of being his wife...

There were layers to me that I had forgotten about
because I was consumed with being the selfless mother
the dying martyr
a withering flower with so much more bloom left
but hidden from the sun...

Growing into a woman with standards
expectations that exceed mediocrity
setting fire to the version of me that
accepted the bare minimum from those who
claimed they loved me
yet always took more than they gave...

I shed old habits like snakeskin
with reckless abandon
overnight, it seems
the word no became a complete sentence
and I learned the beauty of protecting my time
electric fences instilled in my core
ridding me of idle minds that entertain foolishness
freeing up space in my internal memory
allowing me to heal
at my own speed.

DIANA TOWNSEND

Yellow roses
weekly nail appointments
hugs for no reason
delicious meals
I wake up smiling now...
my breaths come softer and slower
no headaches or migraines
I ignore people at will
and explore the selfishness of silence.

I tolerate men
and you will never hear me say
I don't need a man...

I don't need one to live
or to have a meaningful existence on this planet
but there are toils of labor
that pain me
and for that...
yes, I need a man.

Allowing myself to be served
pampered
doors held
feet rubbed
shoulders massaged
chairs pulled out
bags carried
trash is taken out
bills paid

It took me too long to understand
that these are not weaknesses
but the softness of life
that every woman deserves.

Notice the people in your village
who only appear when they need something from you
the ones who only text if you have texted first
friends who never celebrate you out loud
family members who consistently ignore boundaries
people who trauma dump without warning
associates that throw shade with a smile

One by one, pluck these offenders from your life
and acknowledge that some will hurt
like scabs
but you will heal from the loss...

We cannot evolve without shedding old layers.

What takes up unnecessary space in your mind?

In this life, we spend much of our time
searching for love, attention, and purpose
consumed with living life
but unsure about what that truly means...

What is happiness?

People are learning that happiness is not a constant state
it comes in pockets and waves
ebbs and flows in the moments we idolize
and like any high, we chase it relentlessly
but do we ever know when we have actually achieved
true joy?

Your life only has to make sense to you.

Arguing and the absolute headache of
attempting to explain myself or tell my side
of the story...
I don't do those things anymore.

People will think what they want to think
and gasp as you morph into the best version of yourself
ignoring the struggle and hustle
but glorifying the results.

A quiet flex
is sometimes
the best kind.

We don't chase men, anymore
our lives are fulfilled with travel, success, and leisure
our skin is glowing, no longer tarnished with dark circles
marking our exhaustion like a sad badge of PTSD...

Our backs are light now that we've shed the baggage
leaving the toxic men to the sheep who still follow them
avoiding these creatures with more than one baby mama
running from the ones with bad credit
warding off the few who have no kids but also
do not prioritize their mental health...

They say, "Oh, but you will die alone."

Don't tease me with a good time, mister.

Healing is ugly...
wading through guilt
riding the waves of depression that follow the digging
you force yourself to remember the vile things
words that were said out of anger and trauma...

You accept that apologies do not fix
every wound
and that is okay.

Some relationships need to be cut down
like weeds
before they spread and smother
your personal growth.

I was too kind to men
wasting my life on sex that left me unfulfilled
and I didn't experience my first orgasm until
my thirties when I finally took matters
into my own hands...

Orgasms are too magical to be wasted on men
experience one and you will walk among goddesses
streets adorned with gold roses and diamonds
galaxies made of the very being of a woman
the spiritual awakening of a dangerous female
who finally knows her worth...

Do not wait for them to figure out how to get you there.

At what point do we decide
that if someone thinks we are too much
then they should go and find less?

Do not expect someone to accommodate you
when they are intimidated by your excellence.

I feel too young to be with the old crowd
because my bass still knocks until the windows rattle
and my knees still let me get low
my taste in music matches the young folks
and no cap, I know most of the slang…

but…

I'm too old for the youngsters cause
I involuntary frown my face at loud crowds
and I reach for my belt when I see kids cutting up with their
parents cause it couldn't be me and
I blast my music on Sunday mornings when I clean and
my tolerance for bullshit is slim to none and my bedtime
is getting earlier and earlier because
late nights leave me looking rode hard and hung up wet…

This is the weird part of being in your thirties.

Love in my forties
will be calm
southern comfort with a hint of excitement
smooth and subtle
nothing needs to be
announced or declared
there will be no back and forth
I settle into my identity and my solitude
and if you act right, you may be invited in
and you will marvel at the ease
of my presence.

Sage will not clear
a toxic room
if the one burning it
is the problem.

How often do you clean shop?
Erase old messages and delete threads
get rid of pictures or print some for photo albums
go through your contacts and block as needed
manage your friends list and remove the dead space
look through your feed with new eyes and unfollow
any page that isn't feeding your brain...

we are what we consume.

Realization tapped on my shoulder
and reminded me that I have not cried
in a very long time...

Is this happiness? Or maybe just... peace?

Either way, I am enjoying the stability.

Feminine energy is enthralling to me
the softness of being vulnerable
protected and cared for
holding an audience captive without saying a word
the power to cause or end a war
with just a look...

I yearn for the luxuriousness of it all
for I have seen how far nations will go
to capture it.

The idea of friendship has shifted for me
because now I pay attention to how comfortable
people feel
saying disrespectful things about me
to my supposed friends
and I wonder how that comfort was established
in the first place...

Who is arguing with you?

We do not do that here.
My inner goddess does not entertain foolishness
to enter our temple of peace that has taken years
to cultivate and design
arguing with you feels like blasphemy and sacrilege
in this sacred place.

Forty is the golden hour
daring to break the mold
we ache for the chance to slip away
from the edge of mid-life crisis cliches
running from our past and old age
caught in fear as our parents age right before our eyes
hips and knees begin to fail as we pray to the gods
for more time... just a little more time
to finally enjoy life
without social responsibility.

One thing about it is,
I will call corporate,
I'm leaving a review,
and I will call the police on you.

There are clowns out there
but this is not my circus.

I admire the way men will walk away
from any situation that no longer serves them
and I crave the audacity of an ugly man
who sets his expectations high because he feels
he should not have to settle
and I long for the nerve of a broke man
who insists on asking women what they have to offer
besides sex...

Men are fascinating yet simple-minded creatures
and yet, they rule the world.

It makes me laugh until my face aches.

Some secrets
I will take to my grave
and that is the beauty
of this life.

We were never truly meant to know
everything about a person...
and that's why oversharing makes us cringe.

The beginning of each month
I ask the Universe
to remove anyone from my life
who means me harm
or wishes me ill-will
and I ask for clarity and discernment
so I can assist them on their way out
of my life.

Manifestation takes a level of trust
and preparation
because once the blessings arrive
you won't have time to get ready…
once you write it down and set your purpose
the preparation begins in that moment.

Be mindful of what you ask for
and be ready to make room for it
in your life.

Release yourself from the expectations
other have placed on you
they weigh you down
a burden you never asked to carry
and you were never bound to live a version of life
that pleased everyone else
but caused you turmoil and pain.

That simple dedication to keeping the peace
and making everyone else happy
is the only reason some marriages are still going
why some babies were born
and why some of us will never know
true freedom on this Earth.

Permission is an odd word
for an adult.
I don't ask for permission
to do anything
and I insist on telling anyone who will listen
that the only thing I am required to do
is stay black and die.

Like many women
I found myself dusting off the remnants of dirt and shit
after refusing to continue being the doormat for my family.

I sacrificed and endured as long as I could
ignoring my own needs and wants
like a dutiful Proverbs wife should
but I received no blessings for this
and I went feral and scurried into the wild.

Seeking relief and freedom
isolation and peace
exhausted but relieved
because I saved myself from drowning.

I saved myself
from drowning.

Toxic men love listening to you explain
all the ways your exes hurt you
and they take note of how long you stayed
and how many chances you offered.

They gather the notes and make promises
that they would never treat you so badly
they admonish your exes and call them little boys
convincing you that now, yes, now you have
a real man.

Then those men hurt you in ways you never deemed
imaginable
and they recreate the pain from your past relationships
while you ask why, why would he do that to me
knowing everything I've been through.

Baby, you gave him the blueprint
for how to hurt you
and the code for how much
you would take.

A man who does not work,
cannot sleep with me
a man who does not strive to be his best self,
cannot motivate me
a man who mistreats his mother,
cannot convince me that he loves me
and a man who refuses therapy, has nothing to offer me.

They offer crumbs and we pile up like greedy ants,
each fighting for a piece.

So... why are so many of us starved for love?

You are deserving of peace
but I need you to fight for it
claim it fiercely
boldly step into your new position
as the leader of your life.

Your steps may be ordered
and your path might be predestined
but only you can control
how you handle yourself
and how you react to the foolishness
others will bring to your life.

Forgiveness tastes bitter on my tongue
the acid reflux of feelings
I gag on the memories that haunt me the most
and my heart gave up trying to love thy neighbor.

If you hurt me, I will wish the flames of hell upon your soul.

That hill… I will die on.

I have mastered how to smile
and charm my way into spaces
that would've been closed off to me before.

One lesson I have learned is your looks
do not matter
as much as your demeanor and confidence.

Stars aligned so you could be here
so many things could've gone wrong and yet
here you are
in all of your glorious splendor.

May your days be filled with joy
laughter and easy smiles
cleansing tears of relief
healing…
always healing.

The only time I have been loved correctly
was when I learned to love myself
flaws and all.

I had to forgive myself for sins I committed
when I was at war with myself
treasonous acts that went against my good nature
events that cannot be fixed with humble apologies.

I have not always been
the victim.

Black women are the gentle waves of the ocean
the warmth of a plush blanket fresh from the dryer
we are the lullabies of the world
the creation that inspired nations
beautiful and unique
we are the gravitational pull
the solar flares
the world is in the palm of our hands...

Relish in your melanin
enjoy the culture we have introduced to the world
and create your content
continue to share your art
always charge what you're worth
and never ever
give up.

ABOUT THE AUTHOR

Diana Townsend

Diana Townsend is an avid reader and writer who finds joy in the small things in life. She loves to explore the world through the written word, both in the books she reads and in her writing. With a keen eye for detail and a passion for storytelling, she weaves together tales that captivate and delight readers of all ages. Whether you're looking for heartfelt poetry, a sweet children's book, or a thought-provoking read, you'll find it in her work. With her writing, Diana wants to remind people of the beauty and wonder that surrounds us, and the importance of cherishing the small things in life.

BOOKS BY THIS AUTHOR

Black Girl Evolving

Black Girl Evolving is a powerful and evocative poetry collection that delves into the complexities of the black community, mental health, and the vital role of black women in society. Diana Townsend's vivid and raw voice, speaks to the struggles and triumphs of being a black woman in today's world. Each poem is a reflection of the personal experiences of the author, and the universal experiences of the black community. Through the lens of mental health, the author explores the resilience and the beauty of black women, and the importance of self-care, self-love, and self-empowerment. Black Girl Evolving is a must-read for anyone looking to gain a deeper understanding of the black community and the impact of mental health on black women. This powerful collection of poetry is an essential and inspiring read for anyone looking to understand the beauty, strength, and resilience of the black woman.

Things We Can't Escape: Poetry For The Broenhearted

Things We Can't Escape: Poetry for the Brokenhearted is a collection of raw and powerful poetry that delves into the depths of heartbreak and pain. Diana Townsend takes the reader on a journey through the complexities of grief and loss, exploring the emotions that come with being brokenhearted. The verses in this book are evocative and moving, leaving the reader with a deeper understanding of the human experience and the things we cannot escape. This book is a must-read for anyone who has ever had their heart broken.

Love Is For The Dreamers

Love is for the Dreamers, by Diana Townsend, is a breathtaking collection of poetry that celebrates the magic and wonder of love. Written with passion and heart, these poems capture the essence of falling and staying in love, reminding us of its beauty and power. With its sweet and romantic tone, this book will sweep you off your feet and transport you to a world where anything is possible. Whether you're a hopeless romantic or simply seeking inspiration, Love is for the Dreamers is a must-read for anyone who believes in the power of love.

Iced Coffee And Depression

Iced Coffee and Depression is a raw and poignant collection of poetry that explores the complexities of depression and anxiety, the highs and lows of love and heartbreak, and the journey toward healing. Through vivid imagery and candid language, Diana Townsend takes the reader on an emotional journey that is both relatable and deeply personal. Whether you're struggling with mental health issues, recovering from a broken heart, or simply looking for a deeper understanding of the human experience, this book is for you. With its powerful and honest voice, Iced Coffee and Depression is a reminder that you are not alone in your struggles, and that healing is possible.

Made in the USA
Middletown, DE
27 March 2023

27812813R00068